Crazy Campsongs! ™

Dozens of new songs— you already know!

An original collection of new campsongs for kids eight to 80!

By George Petersen and JJ Jenkins
Illustrated by Jack Davis

On the Cover: Jack Davis captures the adventurous spirit of traditional campfire singalongs with this fine illustration of the song "Summer Camp," which can be found on page 15.

Crazy Campsongs!™

By *George Petersen* and *JJ Jenkins*
Illustrated by *Jack Davis*

enpet
BOOKS

First Edition, Spring 2003

Can't find **Crazy Campsongs** in your town? Have your local bookseller, gift or toy shop contact us!
For dealer inquiries, bulk or group sales (including fundraisers for schools and civic organizations), contact JENPET Publishing at Box 2542, Alameda CA, 94501, or visit us on the web at www.crazycampsongs.com.

ISBN Number: 0-9726794-9-9

FILE UNDER: HUMOR
Printed in U.S.A.

Preamble

*O*nce upon a time (this means in the days before video games), the world was a simpler place. People often entertained themselves by singing songs or listening to storytellers weave orbs of magical tales and mystical places. Out of this rich oral tradition came a wonderous musical heritage of madrigals, folk music and spirituals from many lands and cultures. These days, traditional songs—such as "My Darling Clementine"—have little relevance to today's youth, so we created **Crazy Campsongs** as a means of rekindling an interest in that age-old practice known as campsongs.

Along the way, we had some help. We'd like to thank a few persons who helped make this project possible. We owe a sizeable debt to our mothers, who brought music into our homes and encouraged our respective musical directions, as well as our wives who put up with our odd musical ramblings for so long. We'd also like to thank Mr. Jack Davis, who began working on the most excellent artwork for this book in October, 2002—exactly 50 years after the date when he illustrated the very first story in the first issue of "Mad," which debuted in October, 1952. Thanks, Jack—not only for believing in this project—but also for the decades of your wonderful whimsey that has brought joy to millions of fans around the world. You rock!

—The Authors

CONTENTS

the SONGS!

VISIT WWW.CRAZYCAMPSONGS.COM FOR MORE FUN!

ESSENTIALS!

THE TRUTH ABOUT...
CRAZY CAMPSONGS!

Since the dawn of time, humans have expressed feelings and emotions through the use of words, rhythms and music. We now refer to these as "songs," and over the millennia, this has evolved into a fine art. With the debut of **Crazy Campsongs**, some claim that our intent is to defile that art. To these accusors, we can only say: "You betcha!"

To that end, we spent nearly a quarter decade on an intensive research project developing a revolutionary process that will forever change the way music is written and performed. The result is our exclusive "Tuneswapping" method, where the melodies of thousands of existing songs can be used with a new set of lyrics, such as those contained in **Crazy Campsongs**.

New Songs You Already Knew!

Our scientific analysis revealed that a certain common rhyming structure is used in approximately 30% of the songs ever written. It's scary, but it's actually possible to sing the words from "Ballad of the Green Berets" to "The Barney Theme," or the words to "King of the Road" to "The Star Spangled Banner" (or vice-versa). Based on this research, we came up with the "Tuneswapping" formula for **Crazy Campsongs**, the ultimate sing-along book.

THE UNEXPURGATED DISSERTATION

This is the first book of original songs ever published that anyone can perform—without having to read music! If you can read the lyrics in this book, you can sing them to hundreds of familiar tunes, from "America the Beautiful" to "Mary Had a Little Lamb." **Crazy Campsongs** is a collection of fresh new songs you already know!

Get Real!
Most people love sing-alongs, but the problem with traditional songbooks is well... they're traditional. For example, everybody knows "I've Been Working on the Railroad," but get real: When was the last time you saw anyone actually working on the railroad? Songs like this have little meaning in modern society. **Crazy Campsongs** tackles the hard-hitting problems facing today's youth, such as weirdos in the city park, pizza with anchovies, strange little brothers, dog poop on the sidewalks, UFO invaders and disgusting school cafeteria food!

Can't Sing?
If you can't (or won't) sing, no problem. You see, the **Crazy Campsongs** lyrics are ideal for artsy beat poetry readings. Just wear a beret, black turtleneck sweater and sunglasses (or thick glasses), add a bongo player, dim the lights and you'll draw rave reviews. Give it a try!

Not Just for Summer Camp!
Obviously, most people associate sing-alongs with summer activities, but **Crazy Campsongs** has songs dealing with all aspects of life, ranging from school to food, pets and holidays, including our "Generic Holiday Song," which is ideal for any occasion, from Mardi Gras to Arbor Day. As a

This is the first book of original songs ever published that anyone can perform— without having to read music!

bonus, we've included a special "Do-It-Yourself" section for adding your own masterpieces to the **Crazy Campsongs** collection.

Don't be left out at sing-alongs. Get your own copy of **Crazy Campsongs** and start singing today! We'll be listening!   —The Authors

TUNESWAPPING...

HOW IT WORKS. WHY IT WORKS.

Tuneswapping is easy. Rule #1: Actually know the song you're borrowing the melody from. Even with the simple "My Darling Clementine," sing the original a few times before you put our new words on it. Now try the tune with the new words. Easy? Sure, but with all songs, you might have to speed up or slow down some of the words to make things fit. Let's begin with the first verse of "School Bathroom," but any of the **Crazy Campsongs!** would work just fine.

"School Bathroom" (sung to "My Darling Clementine")

In a cavern, in a canyon,
There's one place I hate to go,
ex-ca-va---ting for a mine...
Even though I've gotta go!
Dwelt a min-er, Forty--Niner...
An odor wafts—it ain't perfume...
and his daughter, C l e m e n t i n e
coming from the school bathroom!

Now, let's try something different, putting the new words to the familiar "Deck the Halls." For extra fun, try adding the traditional "Fa la la la la, la la la la" to the end of each line!

"School Bathroom" (sung to "Deck the Halls")

Deck the halls with boughs of holly.
There's one place I hate to go,
'Tis the s e a s o n to be jolly.
Even though I've gotta go!
Don we now our gay a p p a r e l...
An o d o r wafts—it ain't perfume...
Troll the ancient yule-tide c a r o l !
coming from the school bathroom!

There are always a few places where you might have to squeeze or stretch the melody to fit. But make it work, and you'll reach the exalted title of "Tuneswapper Apprentice" in no time!

Get Creative!

Beyond the suggested tunes listed on pages 10-11 to use with **Crazy Campsongs** lyrics, there are thousands more that you can discover on your own. Also, there are plenty of songs where the chorus doesn't fit the **Crazy Campsongs** words, but the verse works perfectly, such as "Yellow Submarine," "YMCA" or "Louie, Louie." You might even try writing new choruses for these on your own! Other tunes, like "Hark, the Herald Angels Sing" or the "Spiderman" TV show theme, work just fine, but you have to repeat the last line to make it fit. Add a little (or a lot of) creativity to your performance, and **Crazy Campsongs** can work with just about anything. One kid even told us she had used our words to Grieg's "Hall of the Mountain King." Scary...

The Passover!

Only have one **Crazy Campsongs** book and many singers? Just go to a nearby bookstore and buy enough **Crazy Campsongs** for everybody. However, if you're hiking in the Himalayas and the local bookstores only carry copies translated into the ancient Sanskrit language, you can still have fun: Simply pass your one book around with each person singing a song to a different tune. On second thought, this may be even more fun with the Sanskrit version!

The Oldest Trick in The Book

Some songs are just too long! If you need more verses, try the old trick used by lazy songwriters: "Third verse... same as the first!" Just repeat one verse (or the whole song) to make the words fill out a longer tune. But our favorite trick with really L-O-N-G songs (like "99 Bottles of Beer on the Wall" or "Row, Row, Row Your Boat") is to start at the front of **Crazy Campsongs** and sing EVERY song, back-to-back. This is a great way to drive your bus driver completely insane on your next school or scouting trip. Best of all... it works!

What's Your TQ* ? (*Tuneswapping Quotient)
CHECK YOUR PROGRESS HERE...

☐ **Wimp**: Thinks sing-alongs are "uncool"... Never heard any really cool ("crazy") campsongs. Uninformed. Out-of touch.

☐ **Tuneswapper Apprentice**: Has sung all this book's great songs to at least three different tunes. Great potential!

☐ **Tuneswapper Deluxe**: Has sung all the songs to five different tunes, added two new melodies to the list (page 10-11) and wrote one new song on page 61. Close to "master" status!

☐ **Grandmaster Swap**: The ultimate tuneswapper! You've sung all the songs to 10 tunes, added six new melodies and wrote two new **Crazy Campsongs**. Only the smartest, the toughest and the coolest ever reach this level. You rule!

TRY SOME OF THESE MELODIES...

Note: There are thousands of tunes that work with the words in this book. Here are over 100 suggested melodies, to start with, but the REAL fun comes from finding some of your favorite songs that work with the lyrics.

A Man of Constant Sorrow
Amazing Grace
America the Beautiful
Anchors Aweigh
Auld Lange Syne
Away in a Manger
Ballad of the Green Berets
The Barney Song
Battle of New Orleans
Be Kind to Your Fine Feathered Friends
Beverly Hillbillies Theme
Beautiful Dreamer
Beethoven's Ninth (Ode to Joy)
Blow Ye Winds
Blowing in the Wind
Casey Jones
The Chipmunk Song
Crocodile Rock
Deck the Halls
Do-Re-Mi
Eidelweiss
Freight Train
From Me to You
Good King Wenceslaus
Greensleeves
Happy Birthday
He's Got the Whole World in His Hands
Here Comes Santa Claus
The Hokey Pokey

House of the Rising Sun
If You Wanna Be Happy
I Love Lucy Theme
I'm Henry the Eighth , I am
In My Life
I've Been Working on the Railroad
Itsy Bitsy Spider
Jamaica Farewell
Jesse James
Jingle Bells
King of the Road
Kumbaya
La Cucharacha
La Tarantella
Last Night I had the Strangest Dream
La Donna e Mobile
Light My Fire
Little Brown Jug
Loch Lomond
London Bridge
Lord of the Dance
Love Me Tender
Mary had a Little Lamb
Mexican Hat Dance
Michael Row the Boat
My Darling Clementine
My Dreidel
Ninety-Nine Bottles of Beer
O Little Town of Bethlehem

Old Folks at Home (Swanee River)
Old Gray Mare
Old Time Religion
O Sole Mio
Puff, the Magic Dragon
Purple Haze
Reuben, Reuben
Rock a Bye Baby
Rock My Soul
Row, Row, Row Your Boat
Scarborough Fair
Shalom Alechim
Sinner Man
Song of the Volga Boatmen
Spinning Wheel
The Star-Spangled Banner
Stars & Stripes Forever
Summertime
Sweet Home Alabama
Swing Low, Sweet Chariot
Take Me Home, Country Roads
Ta Ra Ra Boom De Ay
Theme from The Addams Family
This Land is Your Land
This Old Man
Tom Dooley
Up on the Rooftop
U.S. Air Force Song (Off we go...)
U.S. Marines Song (Halls of Montezuma)
Viva la Compagnie
We Three Kings
What Child is This?

What Shall we do With a Drunken Sailor?
The Wheels on the Bus
When I'm 64
When the Saints Go Marching In
Wildwood Flower
Winter Wonderland
Wouldn't it be Loverly?
Wreck of 97
You are my Sunshine
You are the Sunshine of my Life
You're in the Army Now
Zum, Gali Gali

ADD YOUR OWN FAVORITES HERE!

_____

_____

_____

_____

_____

_____

MORE FUN! A compact disc, with performances of many of the **Crazy Campsongs** tunes, along with instrumental recordings of well-known melodies for creating your own productions is now available. Visit www. crazycampsongs.com for info!

The Zoo

Lots of fun at our town zoo.
Saw the monkeys and the monkey doo.
We ate peanuts, drank lemonade
and found out how zebras are made!

Saw wildebeest and marmosets.
An ostrich ate Dad's cigarettes.
The ostrich died. I guess it's true
that cigarettes are bad for you!

(PLEASE TURN TO PAGES 10-11 FOR A LIST OF POSSIBLE TUNES THESE WORDS CAN BE SUNG TO)

The Heat

There's nothing worse than summer heat.
It makes you sweat and burns your feet.
The asphalt boils and stop signs bend
And people shout: "When will it end?"

The Weather Channel says: "Prepare!
More heat to come than you can bear."
This heat's not bad to me, because
I live next door to Santa Claus!

Summer Camp

When summer comes, it's off I go
to that place where toadstools grow.
The weather's cold. My sheets are damp.
They call this swamp a summer camp!

But this time, it's really great:
We watch TV and stay up late.
'cause alligators came by night
and ate our leaders bite by bite.

(PLEASE TURN TO PAGES 10-11 FOR A LIST OF POSSIBLE TUNES THESE WORDS CAN BE SUNG TO)

The Beach

Day at the beach? This should be great.
Sand and surf—I just can't wait.
The bus ride's long, but I don't care.
I mowed twelve lawns to earn the fare.

As the bus draws closer still.
A sign warns of a toxic spill.
It looks like my summer's over:
The beach is closed until October!

Vacation Fun

For two weeks every July,
we drive and drive: No one knows why.
Truck stop food we're forced to eat.
Bathroom breaks each hundred feet.

Our car broke down, we got a flat
and sister barfed in Dad's new hat.
It looks like rain—wouldn't you know?
Still thirteen days left to go!

(PLEASE TURN TO PAGES 10-11 FOR A LIST OF POSSIBLE TUNES THESE WORDS CAN BE SUNG TO)

Fish

I won fish at the county fair.
We bought a tank and pump for air.
Each cost Dad $19.95...
just to keep those fish alive.

But it was worth it: Every cent
promised years of merriment.
They seemed so happy for a day,
'til little brother flushed them away!

Summer Job

Other kids get crummy jobs,
like mopping floors or stacking logs.
I won't be working at the mall:
I've got the coolest job of all.

I trained hard. I took the test
for "Culinary Specialist."
Now I can wear that paper hat
and ask: "Do you want fries with that?"

(PLEASE TURN TO PAGES 10-11 FOR A LIST OF POSSIBLE TUNES THESE WORDS CAN BE SUNG TO)

The Pool

Kids with pools have lots of friends.
On summer days, it never ends.
Twelve kids are banging at the door,
followed by 200 more.

With mattresses and innertubes,
jet skis, rafts and Evinrudes.
But now, no one's going in.
Some kid peed in the pool again!

Amusement Park

Amusement parks are so much fun.
I begged 'til Dad took me to one.
Roller coasters and Ferris wheels,
Tilt-a-Whirl and junk food meals.

Side to side and round and round,
Dad couldn't keep his corn dogs down.
The whole ride home he didn't speak...
"Hey Dad, can we come back next week?"

(PLEASE TURN TO PAGES 10-11 FOR A LIST OF POSSIBLE TUNES THESE WORDS CAN BE SUNG TO)

The Visitors

Somewhere in New Mexico
the Air Force found a U.F.O.
Somehow those Martians got away.
Just where, the government won't say.

Now aliens are all around:
They've populated half our town.
They've been on Earth for many years.
My math teacher has pointy ears.

(PLEASE TURN TO PAGES 10-11 FOR A LIST OF POSSIBLE TUNES THESE WORDS CAN BE SUNG TO)

Homework

I spend all day going to school.
Sit in the back and act real cool.
The teachers think that I'm so great
because my homework's never late.

After school, I have some fun—
don't worry: My homework's done.
It's finished every day by four.
I pay the kid who lives next door.

School Bathroom

There's one place I hate to go,
even though I've gotta go!
An odor wafts—it ain't perfume...
coming from the school bathroom!

The stench carries down the halls.
The floor's sticky; so are the walls.
What's the answer? Who's to blame?
I wish these kids would learn to aim!

(PLEASE TURN TO PAGES 10-11 FOR A LIST OF POSSIBLE TUNES THESE WORDS CAN BE SUNG TO)

Cafeteria Food

Cafeteria food is so lame.
Day in, day out—always the same.
Brightly-colored: greenish gray.
What is this meat? They just won't say!

It tastes like moldy dog-meat stew,
garnished with some smelly goo.
The milk is sour, the bread is stale:
Our cook should be locked up in jail.

The Big House

Fences high and gates that lock...
I wander through the old cell block.
Watched by an unsmiling face,
I'm trapped inside this awful place.

I know I've got to do my time,
even though I've done no crime.
But soon I know I will be free:
The old school bell will chime at three!

The Big Game

Every year fierce rivals meet:
Two schools—sworn enemies—compete.
We root and cheer our brave team on,
we won't slow down until we've won.

And now the time has come to play.
We shall taste victory today.
Our team's quick moves will win them fame.
Chess is such a thrilling game!

School Nurse

Today I'm dreading my math class,
'cause there's a test I'll never pass!
I "think" I'm ill, I could get worse:
It's off to see the old school nurse!

She sits me down and then I cringe
as she pulls out a huge syringe!
"This won't hurt much—it's for the best."
Now I wish I took that test!

(PLEASE TURN TO PAGES 10-11 FOR A LIST OF POSSIBLE TUNES THESE WORDS CAN BE SUNG TO)

School Bus

The wheels on the bus are always flat.
The windshield's met a baseball bat.
The steering's bad. The brakes are low.
The motor smells in the back row!

To school each morning, every day,
we're always late, but that's OK.
So let's all thank the government
that cut school budgets 10%!

Report Card

My report card's not so good.
It didn't come out as it should.
My Dad is gonna have a cow.
Boy, am I in trouble now!

I wonder what I'll tell my Dad?
To me, it wasn't all that bad:
I got four "F's" and a "D"
At least in Gym, I got a "C"...

Vegetables!

Brussels sprouts and wilted greens,
mushy peas and lima beans,
artichokes and eggplant stew—
Mom says, "These are good for you!"

Turnips and boiled broccoli stalk—
the cauliflower tastes like chalk!
Mom says that I don't get enough...
I've never seen her eat that stuff!

(PLEASE TURN TO PAGES 10-11 FOR A LIST OF POSSIBLE TUNES THESE WORDS CAN BE SUNG TO)

My Room

My parents say my room's a mess.
But it's not bad, I must confess.
I can find my things alright,
though it may take me half the night.

I lift the pile to take a peek,
and found some pizza from last week.
No need to stack my clothes on shelves.
They stand up all by themselves!

My Dog

My dog Spot is my best friend.
We're pals together to the end.
He won't growl. He doesn't bite
or stay up barking every night.

I play with Spot most every day.
He knows tricks like "Sit" and "Stay."
He's just wonderful, you see:
A marvel of taxidermy.

(PLEASE TURN TO PAGES 10-11 FOR A LIST OF POSSIBLE TUNES THESE WORDS CAN BE SUNG TO)

My Cat

We got a kitty yesterday.
She loves to roll around and play.
The other cats don't like her here.
When she comes in, they disappear.

She ate my shoes, she ate my socks,
and then filled up the litterbox.
Mom says her food will cost a lot.
What do you feed an ocelot?

Talking Bird

We bought a talking bird last year:
A single word, we've yet to hear.
We tried flashcards, tapes and books,
yet all he gives are empty looks.

Twelve months of crackers; bribes of seed.
I'm giving up. I must concede.
Why won't you speak? Or won't you say?
His reply: "Parlez vous Francais?"

(PLEASE TURN TO PAGES 10-11 FOR A LIST OF POSSIBLE TUNES THESE WORDS CAN BE SUNG TO)

Rex

Rex is the toughest pet in town.
He growls at all who come around.
He's got the biggest teeth I've seen:
My friends all say he's really mean.

He's got blood-lust in his eyes.
He chewed all my dad's silk ties.
Don't tell the cops: they'll put him down.
They don't like gerbils in our town.

Little Brother

My little brother's pretty weird.
Among all creatures he's quite feared.
He runs his tongue across our rugs
hoping to find some tasty bugs.

In his mouth goes everything
from Kibbles to Mom's wedding ring.
They say this phase will soon pass on.
I wonder where our hamster's gone?

(PLEASE TURN TO PAGES 10-11 FOR A LIST OF POSSIBLE TUNES THESE WORDS CAN BE SUNG TO)

Video Games

Ninja fighters on the screen...
These guys are tough and really mean.
But once you look them in the eyes,
one laser cuts them down to size.

The champion's name on the high score
means fame and glory, evermore.
Someday I will wear that crown...
If Dad would put the joystick down.

Cable TV

We finally got cable TV:
5,000 channels — A to Z.
Mom says some I'll do without:
They've got a code that locks me out.

But I can watch most anything
those forbidden networks bring.
I've got lots of better shows:
Dad's secret stash of videos.

CITY DUMP

JACK DAVIS

42

"Stinky"

I know a kid who smells real bad:
He is quite a stinky lad.
His body odor's rather vile:
I wish he'd bathe once in a while!

He knows he reeks, but doesn't care.
He's never changed his underwear!
But he will get cleaned up today:
The toxics crew took him away!

(PLEASE TURN TO PAGES 10-11 FOR A LIST OF POSSIBLE TUNES THESE WORDS CAN BE SUNG TO)

Our Sidewalks

On the sidewalks of our town,
watch out where your feet go down.
Step carefully or you might find
something a dog has left behind.

One wrong step and you will know
from the aroma down below:
Something awful's on your shoe...
Now you know what doggies do!

Rubberneckers

An accident is in the road.
"Oh look, that car is being towed."
Squealing brakes and fenders mash.
I bet some gawker caused this crash.

As we slow down to gaze and stare,
the cars behind don't see us there.
One hits us first. One more makes two.
The cars now gawk at you know who.

(PLEASE TURN TO PAGES 10-11 FOR A LIST OF POSSIBLE TUNES THESE WORDS CAN BE SUNG TO)

Fast Food

I love the drive-thru. Let's go now!
The kids' lunch deal, I want and how.
The food here's cheap—their ads say so:
$12.95 at the window.

I heard the burger's made with worms,
and soaked in grease to kill the germs.
But I don't eat here anyway:
I want the toys they give away!

City Park

There's a place in my home town
where kids will never hang around.
You'll see nuts and lots of grass...
sandboxes filled with broken glass.

What is this place? Why don't you ask
that weirdo in the hockey mask?
I wouldn't go out after dark
to what they call our city park!

(PLEASE TURN TO PAGES 10-11 FOR A LIST OF POSSIBLE TUNES THESE WORDS CAN BE SUNG TO)

Junk Food

I had nachos and chicken wings,
six tacos and some onion rings,
cookie ice cream—seven bowls—
donuts and ten pizza rolls.

I wonder if I ate too much...
My belly's painful to the touch!
I think this time, I'm really sick:
Hope that ambulance gets here quick!

Movies

I watch movies everyday...
the late show and the matinee.
200th showing? I won't roam!
I call this theater my home.

Drop by sometime and we will meet.
I'm always in this very seat.
Cause sticky cola on the floor
has stuck me here forevermore!

(PLEASE TURN TO PAGES 10-11 FOR A LIST OF POSSIBLE TUNES THESE WORDS CAN BE SUNG TO)

The Mall

Of life's pleasures, large and small,
none beats hanging at the mall.
There's lots of things for kids to do,
when nobody's watching you.

Play with tools to my heart's content,
write my name in wet cement.
A guard yells: "Get outta here—
this mall won't open for a year!"

Pizza

Pizza is my favorite food.
I'm always in a pizza mood.
"I made the call!" I heard Dad say:
The pizza man is on the way!

Look out the window, pace the floor.
He's here! I can't wait anymore!
I love pepperoni and cheese...
"Oh, no... double anchovies!"

(PLEASE TURN TO PAGES 10-11 FOR A LIST OF POSSIBLE TUNES THESE WORDS CAN BE SUNG TO)

52

Halloween

There's one night when witches fly
and ghosts and goblins haunt the sky.
Costumed children walk the streets
seeking tricks and tasty treats.

Door to door, and one by one.
Haunted houses! Lots of fun!
But not as scary as the views
every night on TV news.

(PLEASE TURN TO PAGES 10-11 FOR A LIST OF POSSIBLE TUNES THESE WORDS CAN BE SUNG TO)

Valentine's Day

February brings that special time
heart-shaped cards that say: "Be Mine"
The kids will think I'm "Mr. Cool"...
I've cards for all the girls at school.

I spent all the dough I could earn
hoping for a good return
Now, Valentine's has come and gone...
I didn't get a single one!

A Christmas Wish

Santa brought me everything
Remote control cars that zing,
a Panda playing tambourine
and flying robots—really keen!

Santa forgot one thing, I fear...
I hope it comes before next year:
The only thing I need for these
is 700 batteries!

(PLEASE TURN TO PAGES 10-11 FOR A LIST OF POSSIBLE TUNES THESE WORDS CAN BE SUNG TO)

Fourth of July

July 4th brings parades and bands,
but best of all: The firework stands!
From cherry bombs to rocket fuse—
everything a kid can use.

I took the dough I saved all year,
hoping to buy a souvenir.
My fifteen bucks, the old man takes—
all I got was a box of snakes!

Birthdays

Another birthday. Another cake.
Another cheesy toy to break.
Chocolate sauce poured on the floor.
Where's that ice cream? We want more!

Draw on the walls and kick the clown.
The party must be winding down.
Who's party is this? I've no clue,
but next week , there's one for you.

(PLEASE TURN TO PAGES 10-11 FOR A LIST OF POSSIBLE TUNES THESE WORDS CAN BE SUNG TO)

Legal Disclaimer

There are dozens of special days that don't have a song. With that in mind, our "The Generic Holiday Song" works with any occasion that has a three-syllable name. So here's your excuse (as if you really needed one) to celebrate everything from Ground Hog Day to Mardi Gras, along with Arbor Day, New Year's Day, Guy Fawkes Day, Mother's Day, Father's Day, Boxing Day, Labor Day, Veteran's Day, Bob's Birthday, etc. Incidentally, "roast porcupine" is an honored generic holiday tradition, as very few organizations or governments specifically ban the eating of porcupine on special occasions.

The Generic Holiday Song

When _____ comes round each year.
We decorate with festive cheer.
Such a treat—tonight we dine:
Mom's specialty? Roast porcupine!

Mom bakes and cleans and buys a gown.
Dad makes the punch and drinks it down.
We mark each _____ this way.
Until the cops lead Dad away.

(PLEASE TURN TO PAGES 10-11 FOR A LIST OF POSSIBLE TUNES THESE WORDS CAN BE SUNG TO)

Do-it-Yourself Songs

OK, you've sung all of the songs in this book to each of the 50,000+ tunes written throughout history that happen to work with the **Crazy Campsongs** words. And having made it through those more than two million possibilities, you're bored and want more. No problem! In fact, you can have as many more **Crazy Campsongs** as you'd like, simply by writing your own songs. And to show you we really care, we've provided the following OFFICIAL **Crazy Campsongs** "Do-It-Yourself" pages, where you can archive your masterpieces for the enjoyment of future generations!

Title: _____

_____

_____

_____

_____

_____

_____

Title: _____

_____

_____

_____

_____

_____

_____

_____

Title: _____

_____

_____

_____

_____

_____

_____

About the Authors...

George Petersen & JJ Jenkins

Known for their songwriting/performance collaborations with their San Francisco Bay Area rock ensemble ARIEL, George and JJ have played hundreds of gigs, ranging from small coffeehouses to huge 100,000-person festivals. The two have also produced dozens of records for other artists ranging from rap to jazz, and country to classical. Petersen is well-known for his 20+ years of editorial and writings for "Mix," the leading magazine for audio professionals. Jenkins is a self-taught multi-instrumentalist, musical genius and renowned musicologist. You can hear some of their musical works at www.mp3.com/arielrocks.

Jack Davis

One of America's most beloved illustrators, Jack Davis is perhaps best known for his half-century of work contributing hundreds of unforgettable illustrations in "Mad" magazine and the classic EC horror comics of the 1950's, such as "Tales from the Crypt." Yet over the years, Jack's inimitable style never became tired. In fact, in 2001, he beat out "Simpsons" creator Matt Groening for the coveted Reuben Award bestowed by the National Cartoonists Society. Besides cartooning, Jack's other major works include dozens of covers for leading magazines such as "Time" and "TV Guide," and zillions of record albums, movie posters and book/magazine illustrations.